What Good *Are* Dads, Anyway?

The Value of Dads, As Told By Their Kids

Del Hayes

Del Hayes PRESS

Disclaimer:
Most quotes and sayings herein were taken from various websites found on the Internet. The attribution for those quotes is that of the website. No claim is made as to the accuracy or authenticity of that attribution

Visit our website at www.delhayespress.com for more information.

Hayes, Del
    What Good Are Dads, Anyway? / Del Hayes—1st edition

ISBN   978-0-9822706-7-7
       0-9822706-7-4

Cover design by Clint Hayes
Cover photos and editing by Carole Hayes
Shot by Carole
www.shotbycarole.com

WHAT GOOD *ARE* DADS, ANYWAY?

A GIFT FOR:_____

FROM:_____

OCCASION:_____

DATE:_____

NOTE:_____
_____
_____

Dedication

This book is dedicated, first of all, to all those dads who quietly go about the business of raising their sons and daughters, who seek no attention and no reward for doing so other than the love and respect of their family. It is also dedicated to all those moms who make it possible for those dads to do so.

It is dedicated to one mom in particular, my wife Colleen, the mother of our three children who took essentially all of the pictures herein. Although she is no longer with us, without her being there to record those "Kodak moments," there could have been no book. You may not see her, but she was there in each and every picture, seeing something she knew was important and taking time to see that it was not lost.

Finally, it is dedicated to my own dad, and dad-in-law. Now that they have been gone for some time, I find I miss them in ways that were unexpected. It takes all our lives, it seems, to first understand and then appreciate the effect our dads have on our lives.

A photograph never grows old. You and I change, people change all through the months and years, but a photograph always remains the same. How nice to look at a photograph of mother or father taken many years ago. You see them as you remember them. But as people live on, they change completely. That is why I think a photograph can be kind.

~Albert Einstein

Introduction

What good *are* dads, anyway? It is a question that would have seemed preposterous on its face, generations ago. When much of society was agrarian, dads farmed the fields, tended the livestock, did all those backbreaking tasks that meant the very survival of the family. Dads raised their sons to be men, their daughters to be pure. They worked long, grueling hours on assembly lines, went to war, repaired the car. Dads were essential, the foundation of the family. It was as taken for granted as the rising of the sun.

But not today. There are those who not only demean the role of Dad, but who denigrate the traditional nuclear family. In their alternate universe, males are essential only to procreation, to the continuation of the species Homo Sapiens. Those who believe that, dream of a time when technology and science will make even that role unnecessary. Then society can be rid once and for all of that pesky nuisance, the male of the species.

I am not one who harbors such beliefs. That is true, first of all, because I am a male and not predisposed to fostering my own disappearance. But it is also true because I believe that such attitudes are not just silly and misguided, but destructive to the well-being of society in general and its children in particular.

Much could be offered in defense of the rightful and valuable role of the male, and of the nuclear family. There is far more to being a "dad," than simply fathering a child. A traditional defense could be offered. Several millennia of human history have established the superiority of the monogamous male-plus-female nuclear family. A religious defense could be offered. Major religions all support the male as "head of the household," and often present God as a father figure.

But it struck me, one day, that the best defense of "Dad" would be that offered by those most directly and deeply affected—the children of that dad. So I set about letting them "speak their piece," through this book. Its point-of-view is that of the child. I ask the question, "What good *are* dads, anyway?" and let them answer.

Well, okay—they're my answers, as though the kids in the pictures spoke them. But I believe it is what they would say. I was perusing pictures in our family albums, one morning long before sunrise. I looked at pictures of our own three children, of them with their grandparents. I saw pictures of those children, now grown, with their own small ones. I saw pictures of me with those grandchildren. I looked at those pictures, and thought of what they meant. As I did so, this book came to mind.

The pictures I've included span five generations, old black-and-whites taken with a Kodak Brownie Hawkeye, to modern digitals. But that is part of the message, I think. Dads are links in a chain that binds us to our heritage. Their past becomes part of our present, just as we become part of our sons' futures.

It is said that a picture is worth a thousand words. And in truth, I believe the answer to my title question, "What good *are* Dads?" resides within the pictures I've included. They speak for themselves. I hope you enjoy them.

DH

The most important thing a father can do for his children is to love their mother.

~Theodore Hesburgh

What Good *Are* Dads, Anyway?

The Value of Dads, As Told By Their Kids

What good *are* dads, anyway?

Daddy is a good place to take a nap. He keeps me warm, and I feel safe. I like for Daddy to hold me—even if he is drinking a cup of coffee.

Making the decision to have a child is momentous. It is to decide forever to have your heart go walking around outside your body.

~Elizabeth Stone

What good *are* dads, anyway?

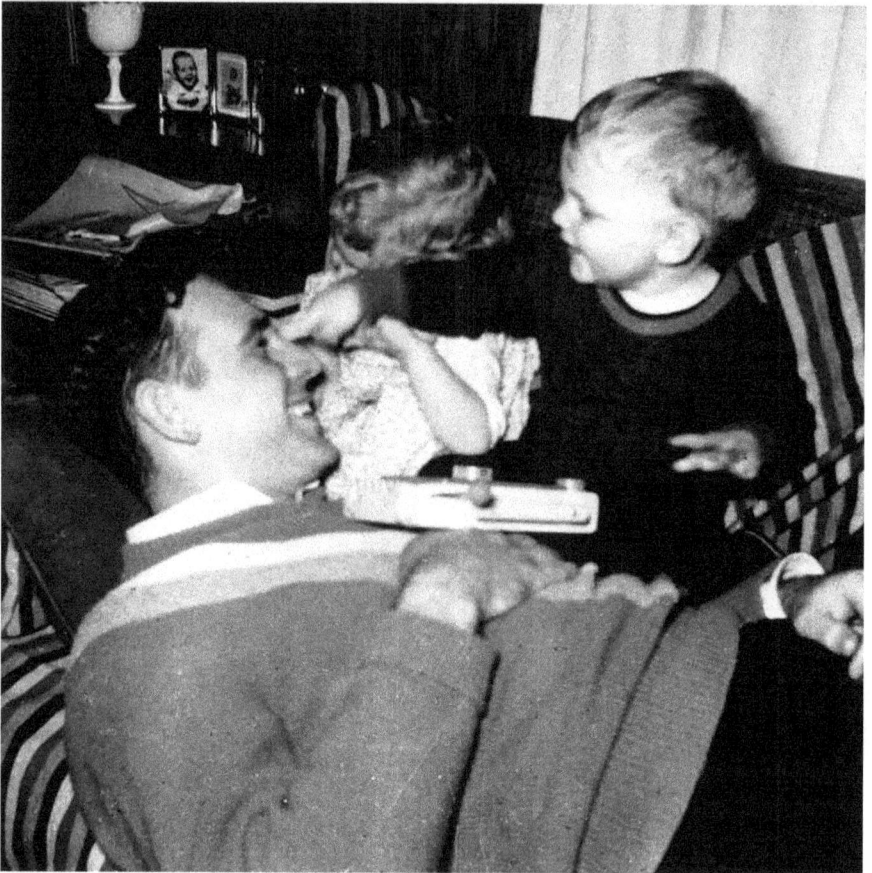

Daddy is lots of fun, and he makes a great toy, too. You don't have to keep winding him up. And daddies don't break, at least very often. They don't even care if you poke them in the eye.

Nothing I have ever done has given me more joys and rewards than being a father to my children

~Bill Cosby

What good *are* dads, anyway?

Sometimes we fuss over who gets to nap with Daddy, but he says there is room for both of us if we dog pile. Daddy is kinda silly. He knows we don't have a dog.

Only a dad with a tired face,
Coming home from the daily race,
Bringing little of gold or fame
To show how well he has played the game;
But glad in his heart that his own rejoice
To see him come and to hear his voice.

~Edgar A. Guest, *Only a Dad*

What good *are* dads, anyway?

Daddy likes to play with me. I like for him to play with me. He makes me laugh, and feel good inside.

Be kind to thy father, for when thou were young, who loved thee so fondly as he? He caught the first accents that fell from thy tongue, and joined in thy innocent glee.

~Margaret Courtney

What good *are* dads, anyway?

Daddy is good at helping me keep from falling down. He holds me up, when I can't stand up by myself. And if I fall down, he's right there to pick me up.

All the feeling which my father could not put into words was in his hand—any dog, child or horse would recognize the kindness of it.

~Freya Stark

What good *are* dads, anyway?

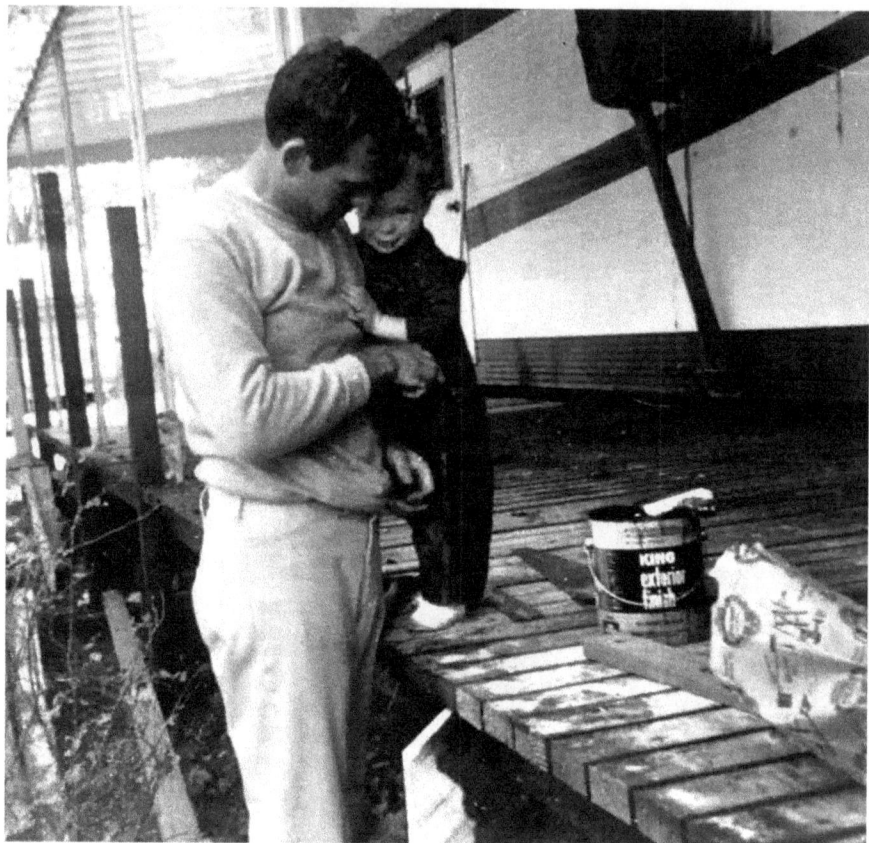

Sometimes Daddy is good for just holdin' on to. It makes me feel better to hold onto Daddy when I don't feel good, or I'm kinda scared. He doesn't care if he's working. He likes to take breaks.

Sherman made the terrible discovery that men make about their fathers sooner or later...that the man before him was not an aging father but a boy, a boy much like himself, a boy who grew up and had a child of his own and, as best he could, out of a sense of duty and, perhaps love, adopted a role called Being a Father so that his child would have something mythical and infinitely important: a Protector, who would keep a lid on all the chaotic and catastrophic possibilities of life.
~Tom Wolfe, *The Bonfire of the Vanities*

What good *are* dads, anyway?

I cannot think of any need in childhood as strong as the need for a father's protection.

~Sigmund Freud

What good *are* dads, anyway?

Daddy teaches me lots of things, like how to work on our car. He teaches me important words, like "ratch-it" and "box-end." Sometimes he gets "owies" and says funny words that he tells me not to say, and makes me promise not to tell Mommy. That makes me laugh.

In the final analysis it is not what you do for your children but what you have taught them to do for themselves that will make them successful human beings.

~Ann Landers

What good *are* dads, anyway?

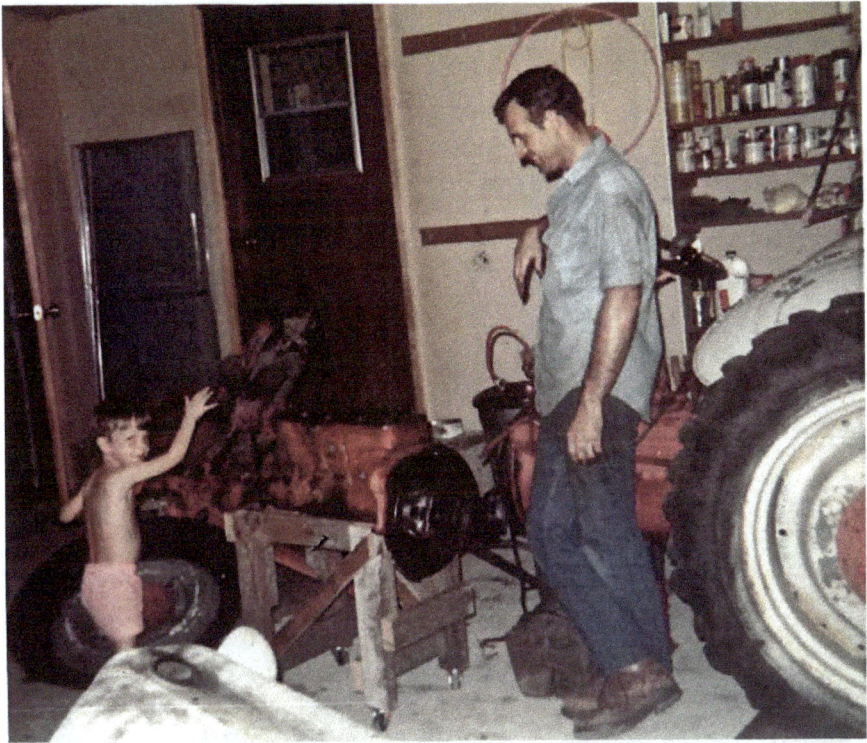

Daddy lets me help him work on things that get me dirty. I like to get dirty. It makes me look like Daddy. Someday I'll be able to work on big things like Daddy works on, because he teaches me how to do it.

He was all questions. But small boys expect their fathers to be walking lexicons, to do two jobs at once, to give replies as they are working, whether laying stones or building models...digging up a shrub, or planting flower beds...Boys have a right to ask their fathers questions...Fathers are the powers that be, and with their power and might must shelter, guard, and hold and teach and love...All men with sons must learn to do these things...Too soon, too soon, a small son grows and leaves his father's side to test his manhood's wings.

~Roy Z. Kemp

What good *are* dads, anyway?

Dad helped me learn how to work on really neat things, like rebuilding my Camaro 350 V8. I added the Hedman headers. It makes me feel good to be able to do that.

The best inheritance a father can leave his children is a good example.

~Author unknown

What good *are* dads, anyway?

The best of all gifts around any Christmas tree: the presence of a happy family all wrapped up in each other.

~Burton Hillis

What good *are* dads, anyway?

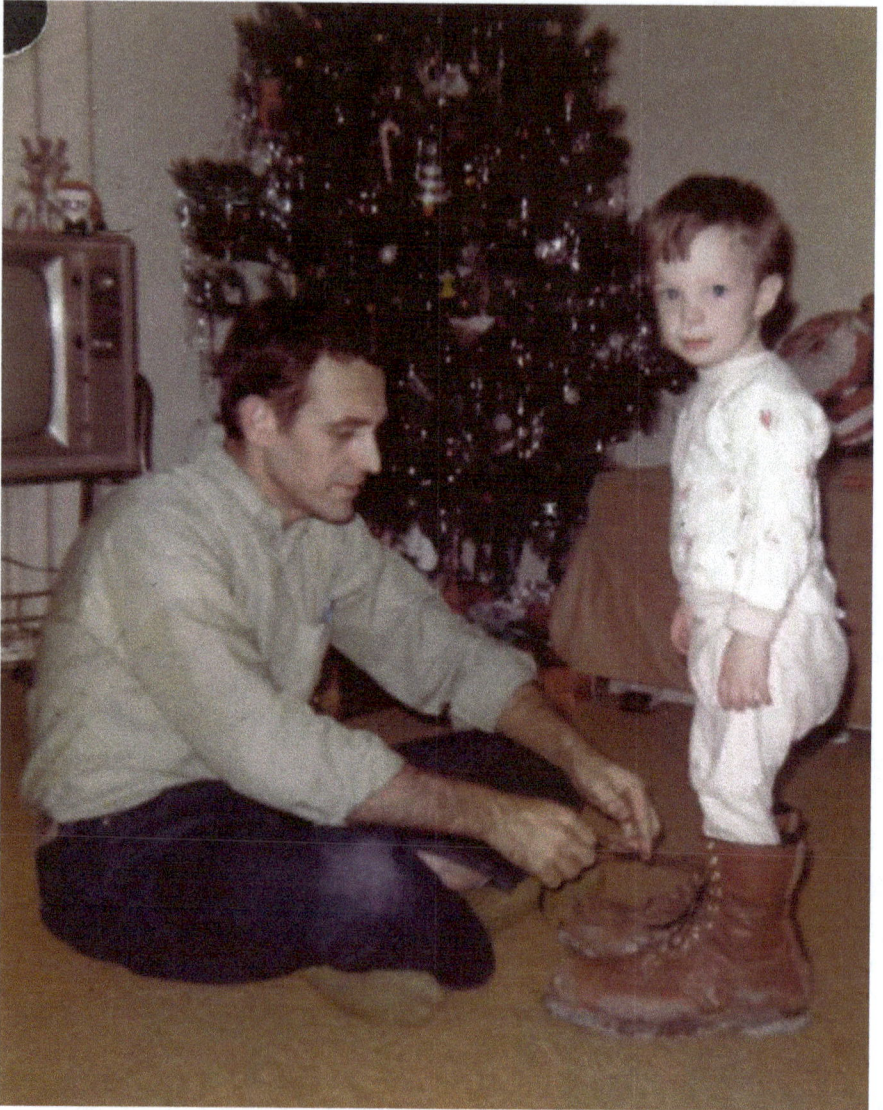

Daddy says that someday I can fill his shoes. I'm not so sure. I think they're kinda big.

There are only two lasting bequests we can hope to give our children. One is roots; the other, wings.

~Hodding Carter

What good *are* dads, anyway?

I like it when Daddy gets the horses saddled. But they are awfully big. They kinda scare me, so Daddy puts me in the pickup, where I'm as tall as they are. I like to ride them, when Daddy rides with me and holds me in the saddle.

What a dreadful thing it must be to have a dull father.
~Mary Mapes Dodge

What good *are* dads, anyway?

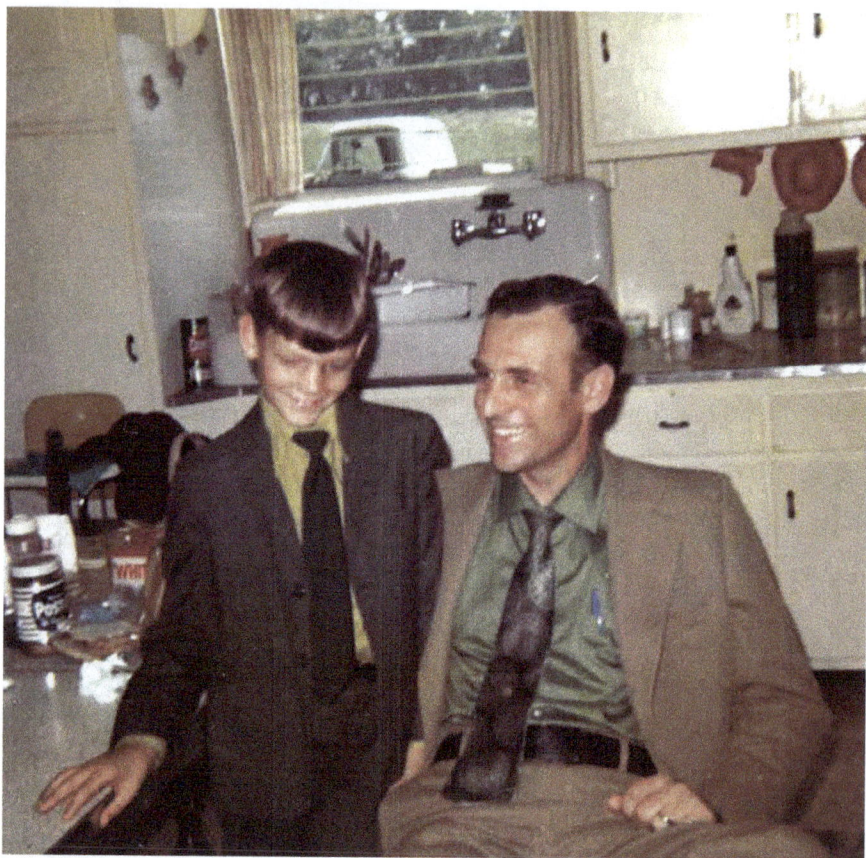

Daddy showed me how to tie my tie. It's kinda hard, because I can't see it, and it's upside down. He still has to help me. I like to dress up like Daddy. Mommy says we both look handsome.

"...somewhere beneath it all Bill felt a sense of pride in the young-boy-turning-man that was his son. He had been a good boy, and Bill knew he would be a good man. And good men knew their minds and made their own decisions. But turning loose of a son was not an easy thing for a father to do."

~Del Hayes, *Ad Astra*

What good *are* dads, anyway?

Dad takes us to fun places, and shows us things that we talk about in school. I like to go places with Dad, because he tells me interesting things about what we see.

He didn't tell me how to live; he lived, and let me watch him do it.

~Clarence Budington Kelland

What good *are* dads, anyway?

Sometimes Dad cries, and doesn't want us to know it. He says that something gets in his eyes. He doesn't like to talk much when he has something in his eye. I don't know why.

The father who does not teach his son his duties is equally guilty with the son who neglects them.

~Author unknown

What good *are* dads, anyway?

No matter how much you grow up, Daddy is still good for holdin' on to—even if it makes him nervous, sometimes.

A daughter may outgrow your lap, but she will never outgrow your heart.

~Author unknown

What good *are* dads, anyway?

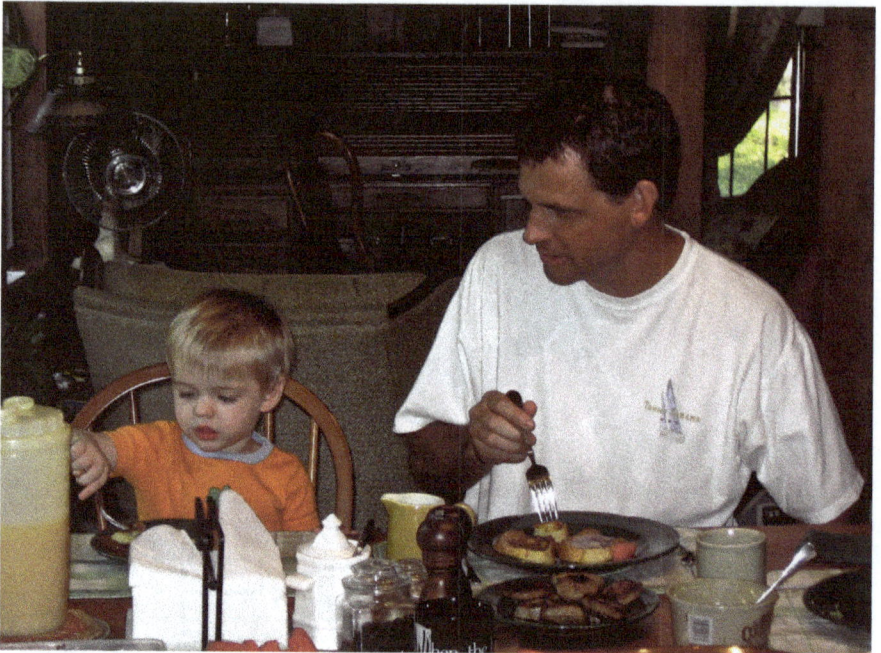

Daddy teaches me little things, too. Like how to hold my fork. I like to be able to eat the way Daddy does. It makes me feel grown up.

Train up a child in the way he should go: and when he is old, he will not depart from it.

~Proverbs 22:6

What good *are* dads, anyway?

Daddy teaches me how to throw a football like a guy, and not like a girl. Girls look silly, when they throw a football.

One night a father overheard his son pray: "Dear God, Make me the kind of man my Daddy is." Later that night, the father prayed "Dear God, make me the kind of man my son wants me to be."
~author unknown

What good *are* dads, anyway?

Daddy helps me learn how to use the computer. It makes me laugh when Daddy says "Google it."

A man's worth is measured by how he parents his children. What he gives them, what he keeps away from them, the lessons he teaches and the lessons he allows them to learn on their own.

~Lisa Rogers

What good *are* dads, anyway?

I like it when Daddy lets me help him work. It makes me feel important.

When it comes to little girls, God the father has nothing on father, the god. It's an awesome responsibility.

~Frank Pittman

What good *are* dads, anyway?

Daddy is strong, and can play lots of games that Mommy can't play, like how to ride a bucking bronco.

Home ain't a place that gold can buy,
or get up in a minute;
Afore it's home there's got t' be
a heap o' livin' in it;
Within the walls there's got t' be
some babies born, and then
right there ye've got t' bring 'em up
t' women good, and men;

~Edgar A. Guest, *Home*

What good *are* dads, anyway?

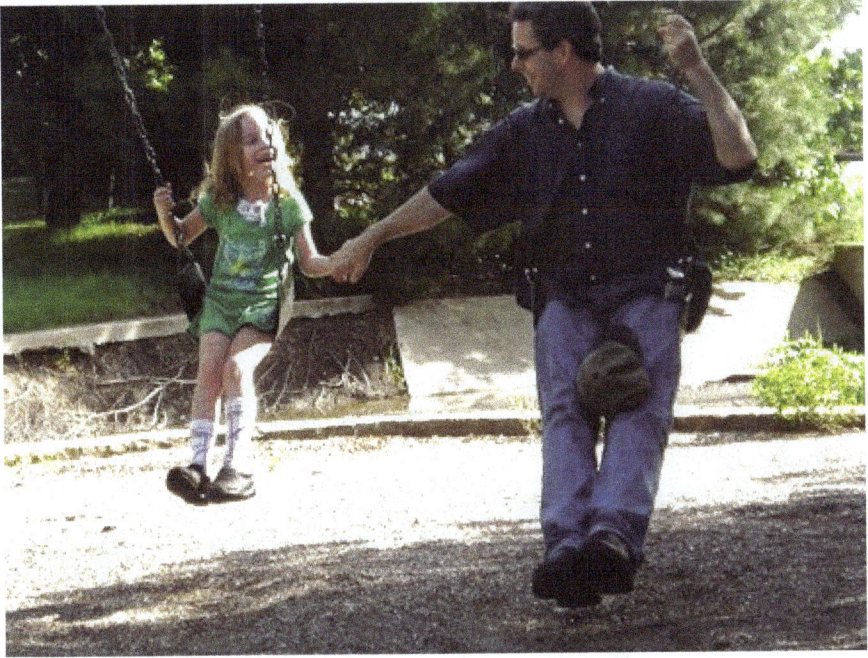

If you can give your son or daughter only one gift, let it be enthusiasm.

~Bruce Barton

What good *are* dads, anyway?

I like to play ball with Daddy. He shows me how to hold my bat, and says "good hit!" when I hit it. He doesn't care if he has to chase the ball, even if I miss it. I think Daddy likes to play ball with me, too.

My father used to play with my brother and me in the yard. Mother would come out and say, "You're tearing up the grass." "We're not raising grass," my dad would reply, "we're raising boys."
~Harmon Killebrew

What good *are* dads, anyway?

We always like it when Daddy takes us all shopping. It's a lot of fun. Daddy even says it's fun for him. I don't know if it is, really, or if he just says that to make Mommy feel good.

It is admirable for a man to take his son fishing, but there is a special place in heaven for the father who takes his daughter shopping.

~John Sinor

What good *are* dads, anyway?

Certain is it that there is no kind of affection so purely angelic as of a father to a daughter. In love to our wives there is desire; to our sons, ambition; but to our daughters there is something which there are no words to express.

~ Joseph Addison

What good *are* dads, anyway?

Dads are good for just talkin' to. It doesn't seem to matter how old you are.

My father gave me the greatest gift anyone could give another person—he believed in me.

~Jim Valvano

What good *are* dads, anyway?

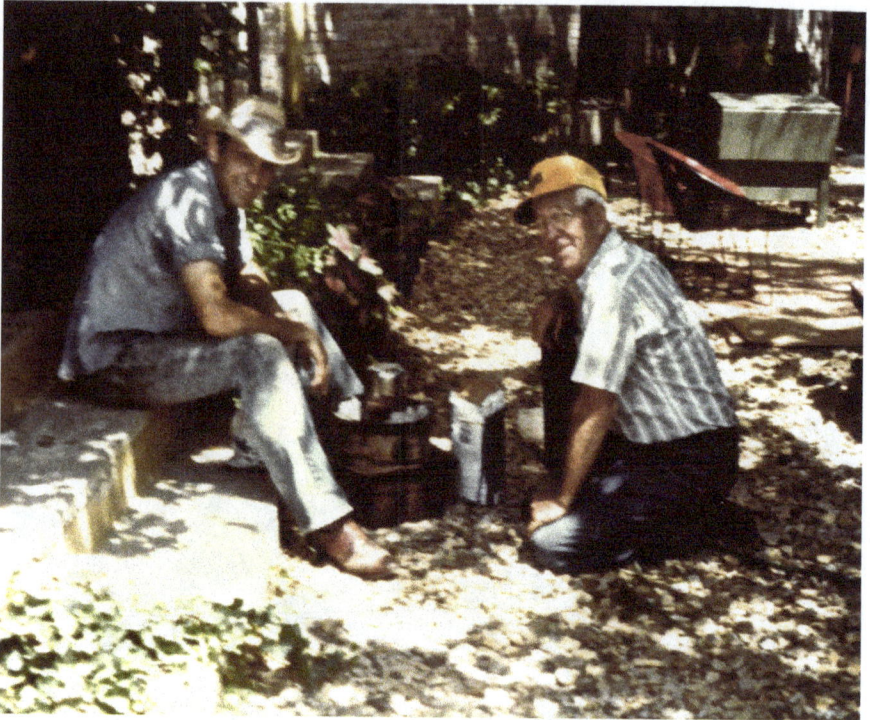

Especially if we're talkin' over an ice cream freezer.

Until you have a son of your own...you will never know the joy, the love beyond feeling that resonates in the heart of a father as he looks upon his son. You will never know the sense of honor that makes a man want to be more than he is and to pass something good and hopeful into the hands of his son. And you will never know the heartbreak of the fathers who are haunted by the personal demons that keep them from being the men they want their sons to be.

~Kent Nerburn

What good *are* dads, anyway?

After a long time, daddies get to graduate and be "Grand" dads. Then they are really special, because they have more time, and they spoil you. They let us do important things, too, like carrying the milk pail from the barn.

My grandfather once told me that there are two kinds of people: those who work and those who take the credit. He told me to try to be in the first group; there was less competition there.

~Indira Ghandi

What good *are* dads, anyway?

Granddad teaches me how to fish. Granddad likes to go fishing. I'm glad he takes me with him. It's really fun, 'specially when we catch big ones.

There are fathers who do not love their children; there is no grandfather who does not adore his grandson.

~Victor Hugo

What good *are* dads, anyway?

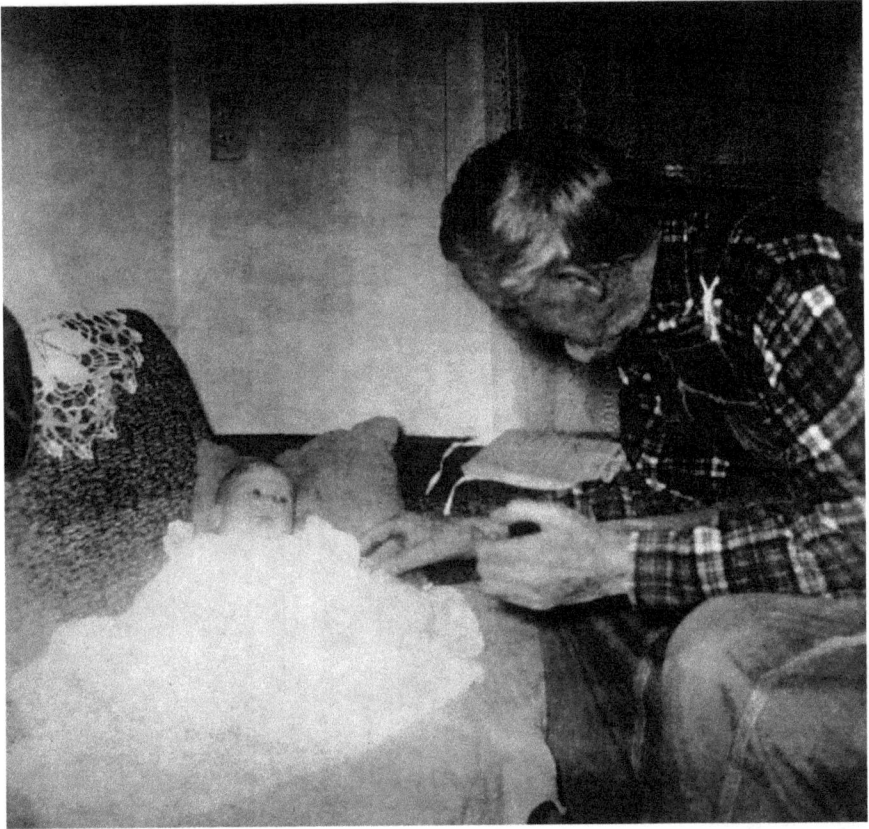

A grandfather is someone with silver in his hair and gold in his heart.

~Author unknown

What good *are* dads, anyway?

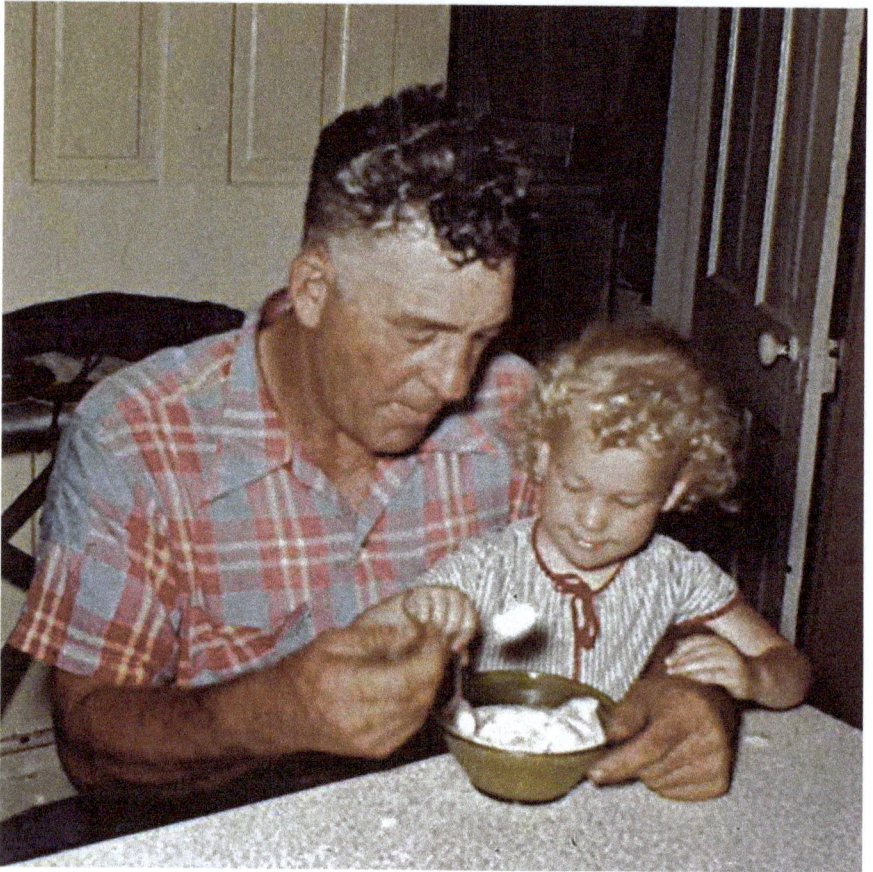

Grandpa likes to eat ice cream. So do I, but it's slippery and falls off my spoon, unless Grandpa helps me a little. But he doesn't mind, I think.

Nobody can do for little children what grandparents do. Grandparents sort of sprinkle stardust over the lives of little children.

~Alex Haley

What good *are* dads, anyway?

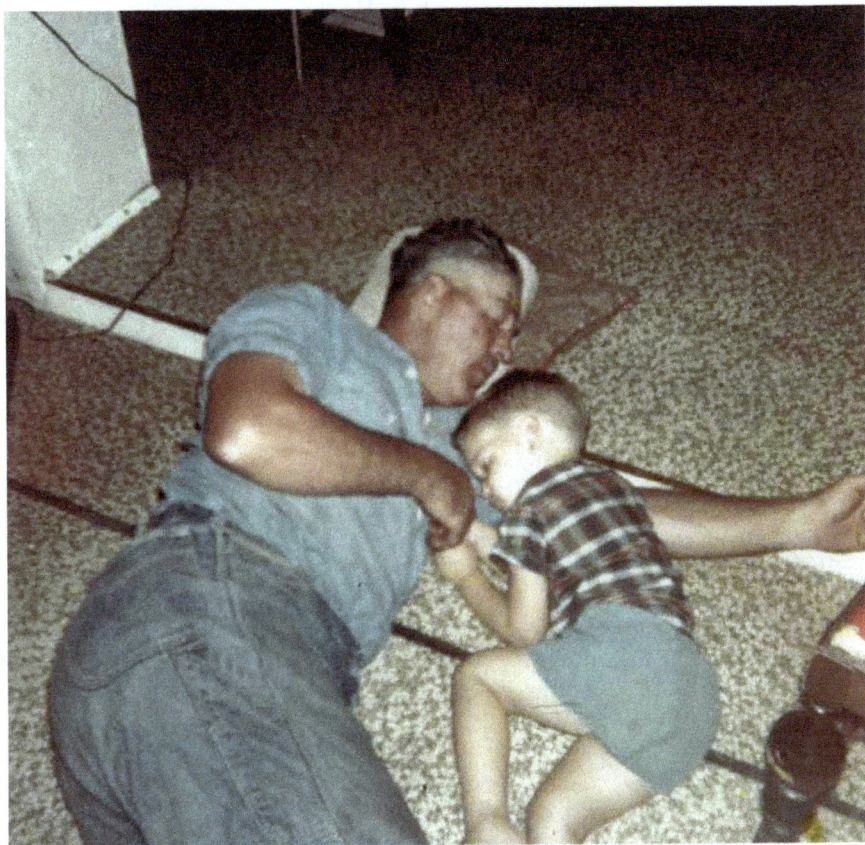

Grandpa says us men-folk need our naps, after a morning of hard work. I think he's right.

People will not look forward to posterity who never look backward to their ancestors.

~Edmund Burke

What good *are* dads, anyway?

It's one of nature's ways that we often feel closer to distant generations than to the generation immediately preceding us.
~Igor Stravinsky

What good *are* dads, anyway?

Granddad showed me the right way to hold the screwdriver, and turn it. He says I'm a pretty good mechanic.

You've got to do your own growing, no matter how tall your grandfather was.

~Irish Proverb

What good *are* dads, anyway?

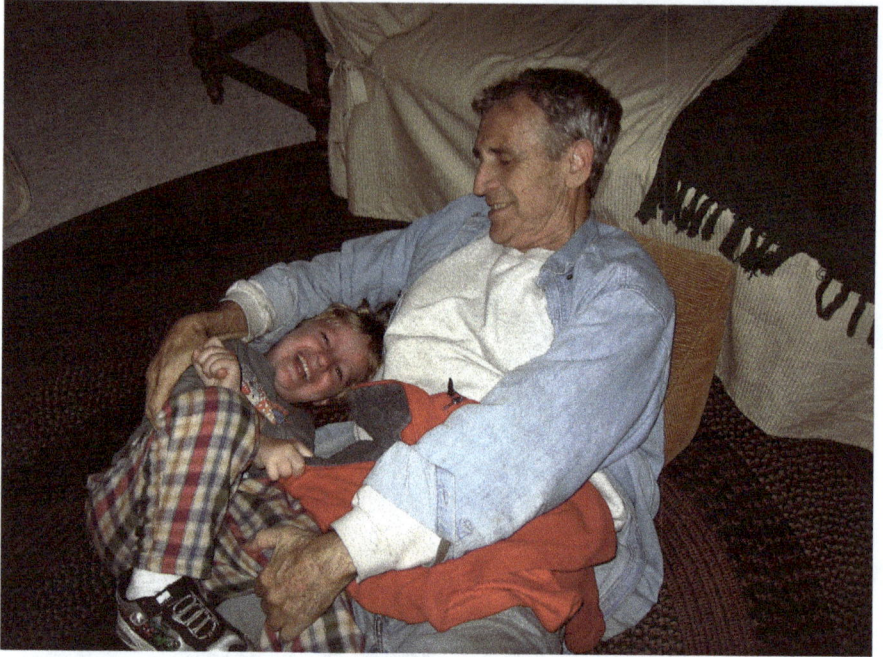

You don't quit laughing because you grow old, you grow old because you stop laughing.

~Author unknown

What good *are* dads, anyway?

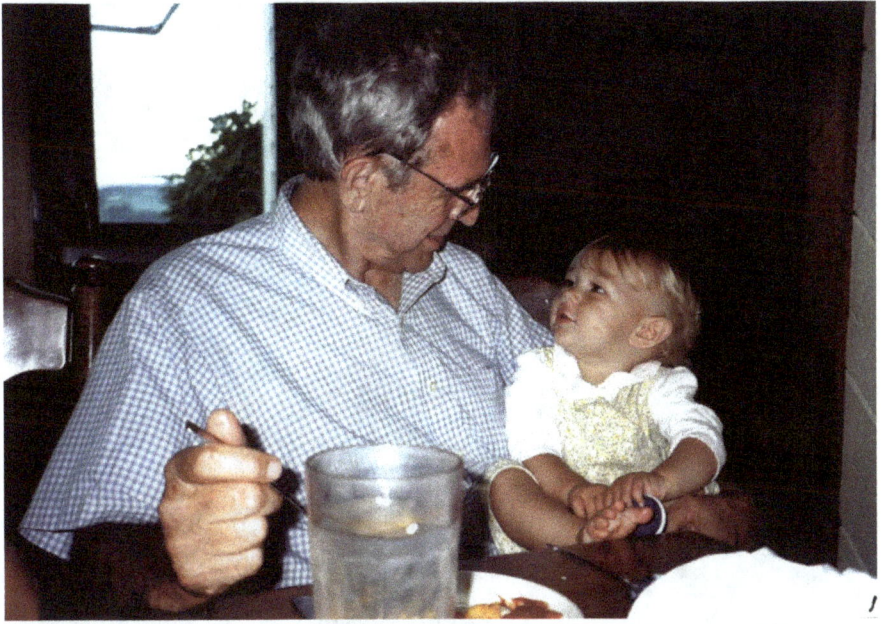

Granddad is fun to talk to. He has lots of funny stories. And he feeds me cherry pie and ice cream, even if I haven't eaten all my vegetables.

I'm going to be your grandpa!! I have the biggest smile. I've been waiting to meet you for such a long, long while.

~Billy Crystal

What good *are* dads, anyway?

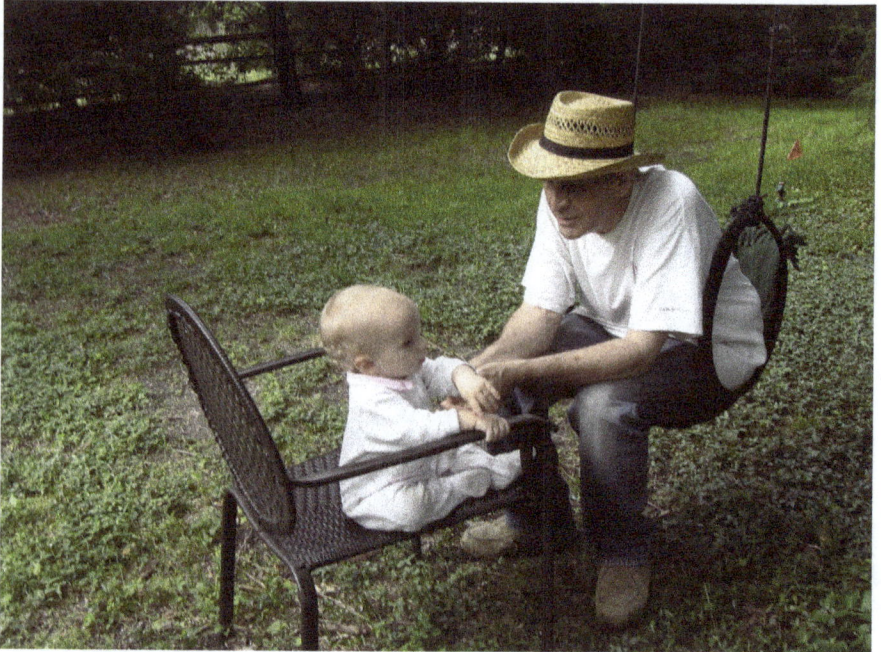

Granddad likes to just sit and talk. He doesn't seem to really care if I don't have a whole lot to say.

If I had known how wonderful it would be to have grandchildren, I'd have had them first.

~Lois Wyse

What good *are* dads, anyway?

Granddad said he couldn't have finished this table without my help. I like to help Granddad.

Grandfathers are for loving and fixing things.
~Author unknown

What good *are* dads, anyway?

Granddad said "I'm not sure I've got lap enough for all three of you," but I said, "Sure you do, Granddad. See?"

Few things are more delightful than grandchildren fighting over your lap.

~Doug Larson

What good *are* dads, anyway?

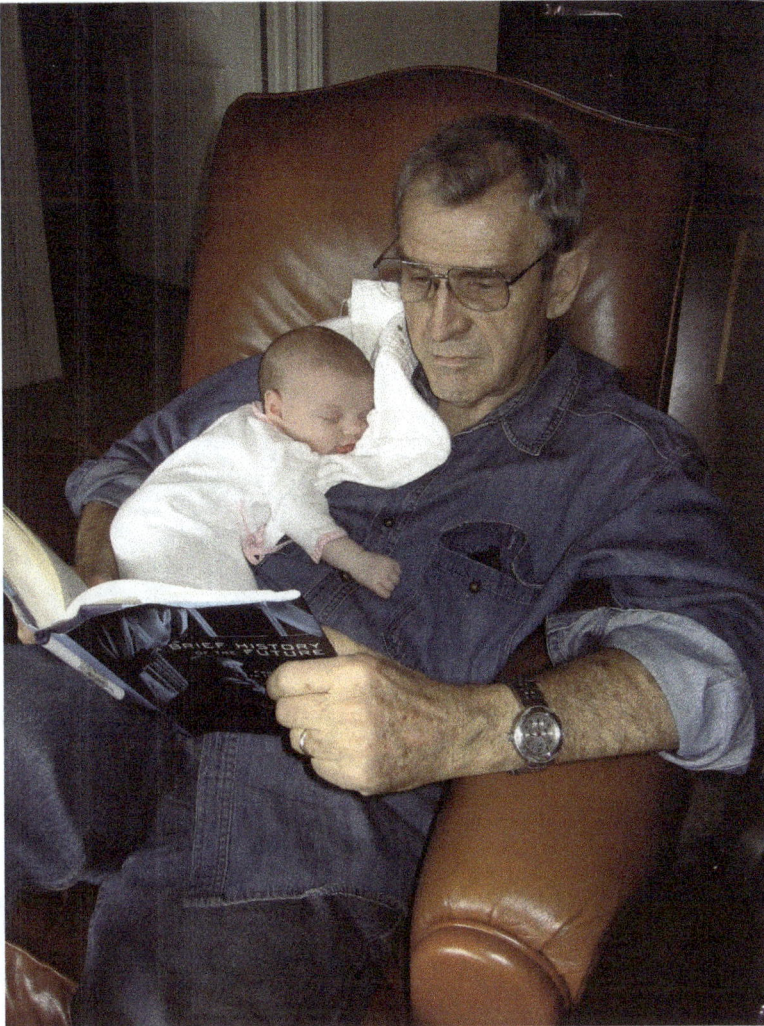

Sometimes I feel fussy, and don't want to take my naps. But it's easy to take my nap when Granddad holds me. It feels good. I think he's done it before.

One of the most powerful handclasps is that of a new grandbaby around the finger of a grandfather.
                                                    ~Joy Hargrove

What good *are* dads, anyway?

Granddad said he'd teach me how to drive the tractor, but I'm a little scared of it. It's awfully loud.

The history of our grandparents is remembered not with rose petals but in the laughter and tears of their children and their children's children. It is into us that the lives of grandparents have gone. It is in us that their history becomes a future.
~Charles and Ann Morse

What good *are* dads, anyway?

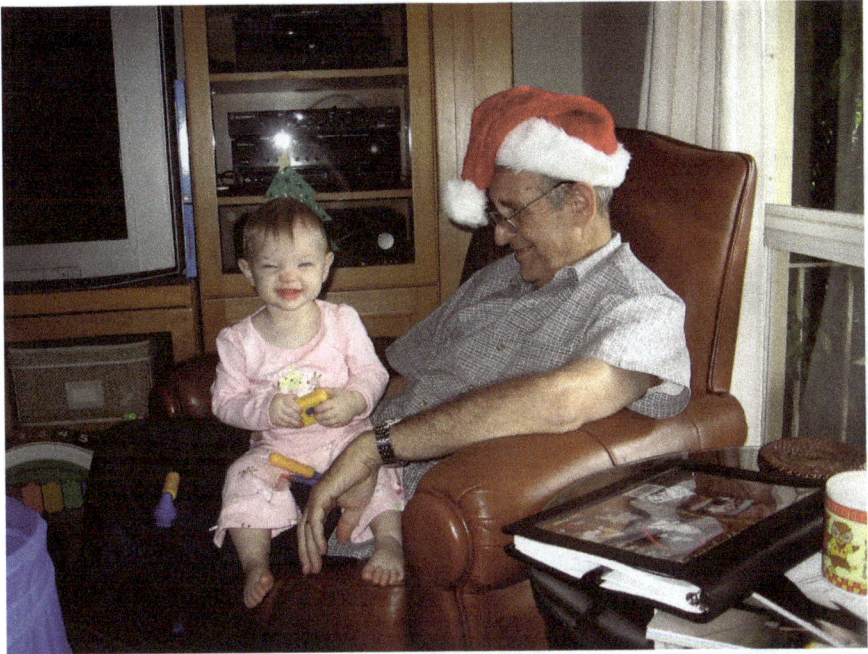

Granddad wants me to believe that he's Santa Claus. Silly Granddad. He's not fat enough, and besides, he lives in Texas. Everybody knows Santa Claus lives at the North Pole, with Rudolph.

Being grandparents sufficiently removes us from the responsibilities so that we can be friends.

~ Allan Frome

What good *are* dads, anyway?

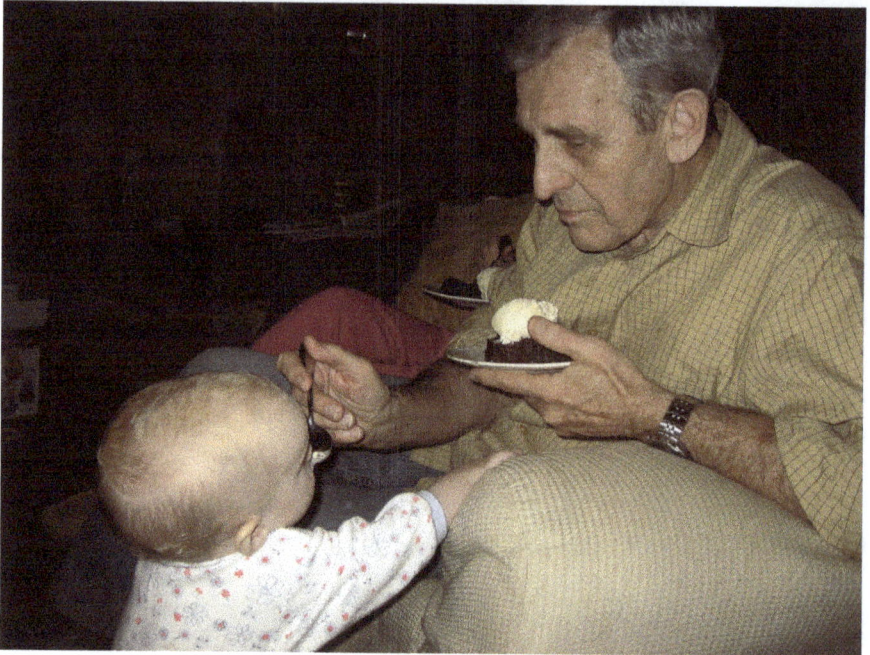

What children need most are the essentials that grandparents provide in abundance. They give unconditional love, kindness, patience, humor, comfort, lessons in life. And, most importantly, cookies.

~Rudolph Giuliani

What good *are* dads, anyway?

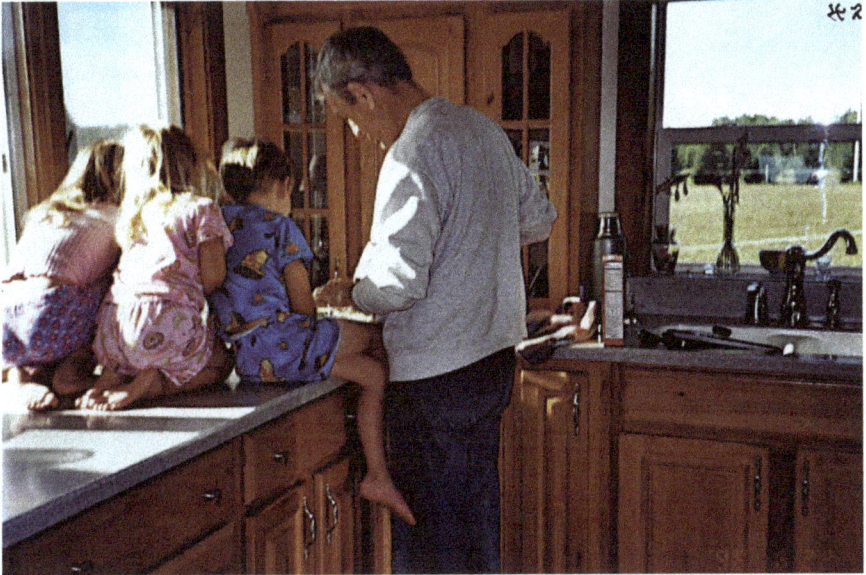

That's all, folks. We've got work to do.

Heaven's mighty fine, I know . . .
Still, it ain't so bad here.
See them maples all aglow;
Starlings seem so glad here:
I'll be mighty peeved to go,
Scrumptious times I've had here.

~Robert William Service, *Granddad*

www.ingramcontent.com/pod-product-compliance
Lightning Source LLC
Chambersburg PA
CBHW070828100426
42813CB00003B/535